THE NEW STARLIGHT EXPRESS
VOCAL SELECTIONS

Exclusive Distributors:
Music Sales Limited, 8/9 Frith Street, London W1V 5TZ, England.

Order No. RG10195
ISBN 0-7119-3603-X

Photographs by Nobby Clarke.

This edition © 1993 The Really Useful Group Limited.

A REALLY USEFUL GROUP PUBLICATION

MUSIC BY
ANDREW LLOYD WEBBER

LYRICS BY
RICHARD STILGOE

DESIGNED BY
JOHN NAPIER

CHOREOGRAPHY BY
ARLENE PHILLIPS

LIGHTING BY
DAVID HERSEY

SOUND BY
MARTIN LEVAN

PRODUCTION MUSICAL DIRECTOR
DAVID CADDICK

ORIGINAL ORCHESTRATION BY
ANDREW LLOYD WEBBER & DAVID CULLEN

1993 ORCHESTRATION BY
ANDREW LLOYD WEBBER, NIGEL WRIGHT & DAVID CULLEN

DIRECTED BY
TREVOR NUNN

PRODUCED BY THE REALLY USEFUL THEATRE COMPANY LIMITED
'NEXT TIME YOU FALL IN LOVE' LYRICS BY DON BLACK

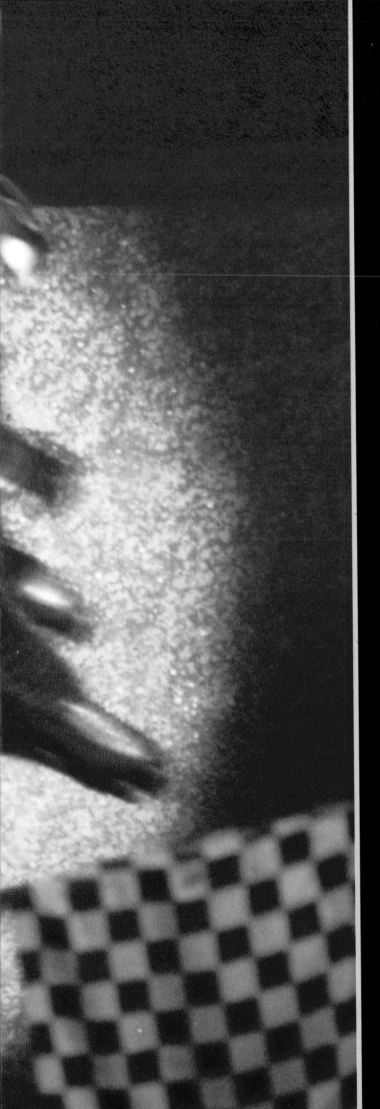

STARLIGHT EXPRESS

Starlight Express began life in 1973. I was asked to compose the music for a series of cartoons for television based on the Thomas the Tank Engine stories.

Two years later my life was complicated by meeting a soul singer who had the unusual gift of being able to sing three notes at once in the exact pitch of an American steam whistle. Meanwhile, I had been approached by another television company about a cartoon version of Cinderella. Soon it became a Cinderella story about trains. A famous Prince was to hold a competition to decide which engine would pull the royal train across the United States of America. Cinderella was a steam engine, the ugly sisters were to be a diesel and an electric.

The steam engine won the competition with a little help from the Fairy Godmother... The Midnight Special (The Starlight Express). The Midnight Train lent the steam engine special equipment on condition it was all back by midnight, so the Special could leave on time. In his haste to get back on time the steam engine dropped a piston. The Prince went around America to find the engine which the piston fitted, etc., etc.

The project never got off the ground! In the summer of 1982 I took my young son, Nicholas, to the Valley Railroad en route to the Goodspeed Opera House in Connecticut. I shall never forget his face of pure joy and amazement when the big American steam locomotive arrived.

So at the 1982 Sydmonton Festival Starlight was finally performed with the intention that it might become a concert for schools. Here it was heard by Trevor Nunn. First there was a plan that it should open the new Barbican Centre in London as a concert sung by all the schools of the City of London, but the ever-resourceful Mr Nunn had other ideas. He felt that the story should be more about competition, that for children today it should be more of a pop score and above all that it could be a staged "event" because trains could happen through roller skates. Frankly, some of us had doubts so the first act was "workshopped" in 1983. The London production of Starlight Express opened in March 1984.

This year the entire creative team came together again to re-produce the show for a new generation. There are five new songs. They are featured in the completely new recording of the show.

Andrew Lloyd Webber 1993

ROLLING STOCK

MUSIC BY ANDREW LLOYD WEBBER
LYRICS BY RICHARD STILGOE

I'm just the fast-est thing you'll
Don't try to show you can go

ev - er see,___ that streak of light-ning you just missed was me,___
fast - er than me,___ this is my back view and it's all you'll see,___

don't stop now, we got-ta keep it go-ing all night.___
don't stop now, we got-ta keep it go-ing all night.___

[6]

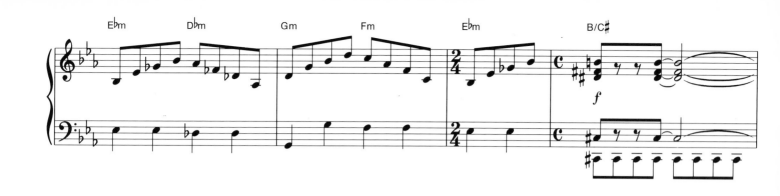

So get the mo-tion in your wheels some-how, the rac-ing ac-tion's start-ing here and now,

don't stop now, we got-ta keep it go-ing all night. _

HE'LL WHISTLE AT ME

MUSIC BY ANDREW LLOYD WEBBER
LYRICS BY RICHARD STILGOE

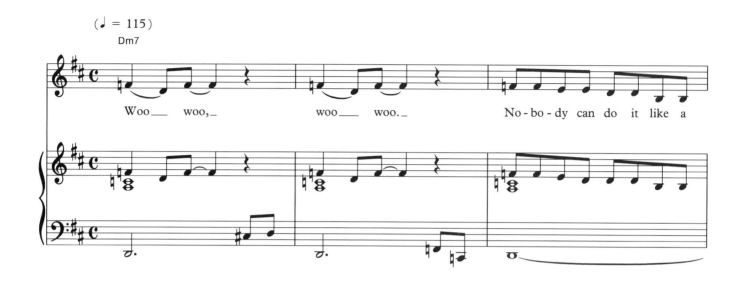

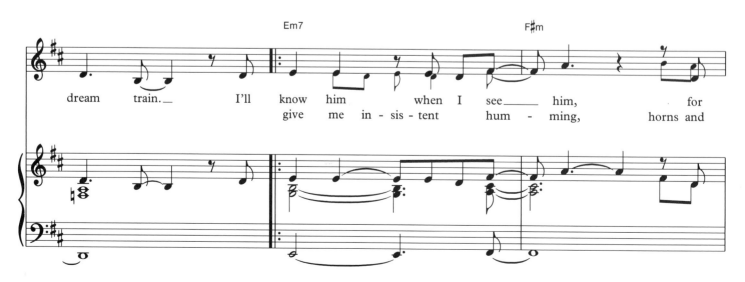

AC/DC

MUSIC BY ANDREW LLOYD WEBBER
LYRICS BY RICHARD STILGOE

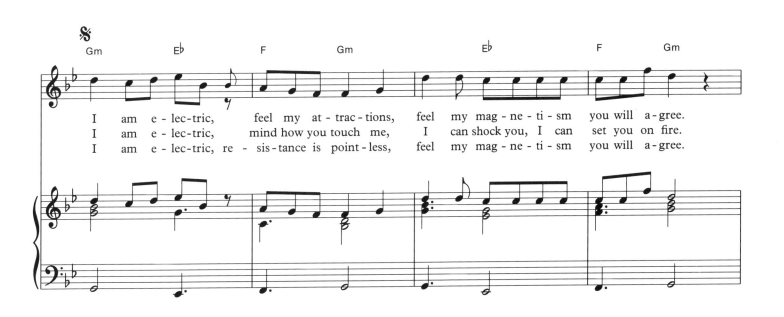

I am e-lec-tric, feel my at-trac-tions, feel my mag-ne-ti-sm you will a-gree.
I am e-lec-tric, mind how you touch me, I can shock you, I can set you on fire.
I am e-lec-tric, re-sis-tance is point-less, feel my mag-ne-ti-sm you will a-gree.

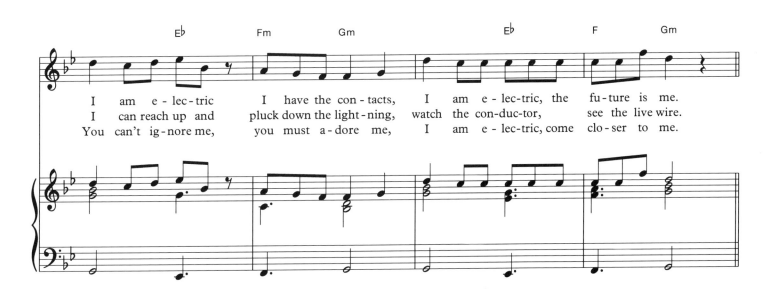

I am e-lec-tric I have the con-tacts, I am e-lec-tric, the fu-ture is me.
I can reach up and pluck down the light-ning, watch the con-duc-tor, see the live wire.
You can't ig-nore me, you must a-dore me, I am e-lec-tric, come clo-ser to me.

PUMPING IRON

MUSIC BY ANDREW LLOYD WEBBER
LYRICS BY RICHARD STILGOE

Lis - ten to the chat - ter of the die - sel__ force, ge - ne - ra - ting twen - ty se - ven
Ev - ery-bo - dy's gon - na say that train is__ smart, the migh - ty die - sel en - gine is a

hun - dred horse, cam - shaft rol - ling while the rock - ers__ rock,__ hear me
work of__ art,__ the un - dis-pu - ted lead - er of the roll - ing__ stock,__ now see me

knock. See me hus - tle, feel my mus - cle
rock. See me hus - tle, feel my mus - cle,

pump - ing iron._____ Trying to build my bo - dy,__
pump - ing iron._____ Stretch - ing my bull - work - er,__

Hey - ey - ey - ey. Head - ing for the ral - ly, __ (Head - ing for the ral - ly,) __

Gon - na win the first race __ (Gon - na win the first race.) gon - na run the long - est, the

big - gest and the strong - est, I'm knock - ing, said I'm knock - ing, you know I'm

knock - ing, knock! I'm pump - ing iron.

CRAZY

MUSIC BY ANDREW LLOYD WEBBER
LYRICS BY RICHARD STILGOE

Where I go the rest____ bet-ter fol-low, look out ev-ery-bo-dy move a -
Watch me, see me hit____ that ho-ri-zon, take it slow-ly, what you got to

- side. May go now or may go to-mor-row, hold on, I'll
prove? Ride with me, you'll know you've been ri-ding, no - one can

oo wa wa wa wa.

Hold on tight I'll turn up the pres-sure, must be right, no way it can be

wrong. You and me go steam - ing to - ge-ther,

till some - one bet - ter comes a - long.

[25]

MAKE UP MY HEART

MUSIC BY ANDREW LLOYD WEBBER
LYRICS BY RICHARD STILGOE

It's time to choose be-tween the two of them, I'd bet-ter make a start.
I don't want one to win and one to lose, can't tell them yes or no.

Some-one help me make up my heart,___ tell me how to make up my heart.___
Choos-ing one means let-ting one go,___ I can't face let-ting one of them go.___

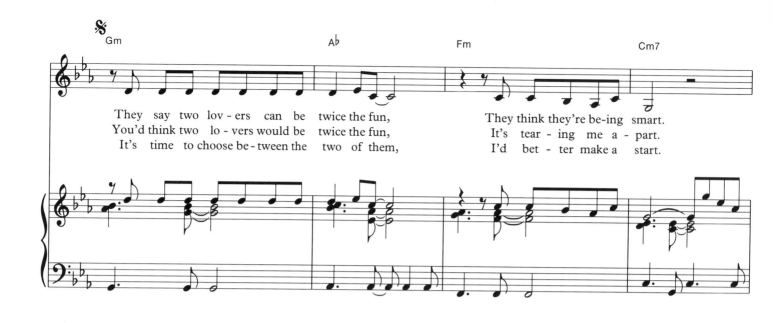

They say two lov-ers can be twice the fun, They think they're be-ing smart.
You'd think two lo-vers would be twice the fun, It's tear-ing me a-part.
It's time to choose be-tween the two of them, I'd bet-ter make a start.

Some-one help me make up my heart,_ please tell me how to make up my heart._
Some-one help me make up my heart,_ please tell me how to make up my heart._
Some-one help me make up my heart,_ please tell me how to make up my heart._

(1.) One of them is strong, one of them is good, but both could turn out wrong, so who gets the
(2. 3.) One of them has style, sets the world a-light, the oth-er makes me smile, so who gets the

[29]

U.N.C.O.U.P.L.E.D.

MUSIC BY ANDREW LLOYD WEBBER
LYRICS BY RICHARD STILGOE

to Coda ⊕

marriage, I'm a van without a man, I've been U. N. C. O. U. P. L. E.
think, "There she goes, the missing link, she's been U. N. C. O. U. P. L. E.

D. Was I corroded, or overloaded? Maybe I

shamed him, who would have blamed him, if he thought me second

class, went in search of chrome and brass, went to find some other fool like

STARLIGHT SEQUENCE

MUSIC BY ANDREW LLOYD WEBBER
LYRICS BY RICHARD STILGOE

Star-light ex - press. _____

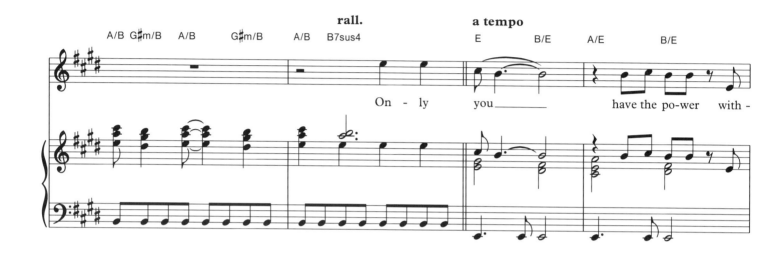

On - ly you____ have the po-wer with -

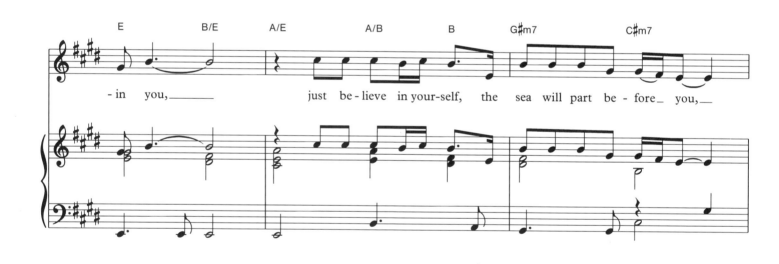

- in you,____ just be - lieve in your-self, the sea will part be - fore_ you,__

stop the rain and turn the tide.____ If on - ly you____

look in your mind, I'm there, ____ no-thing's new. The star-light ex - press is

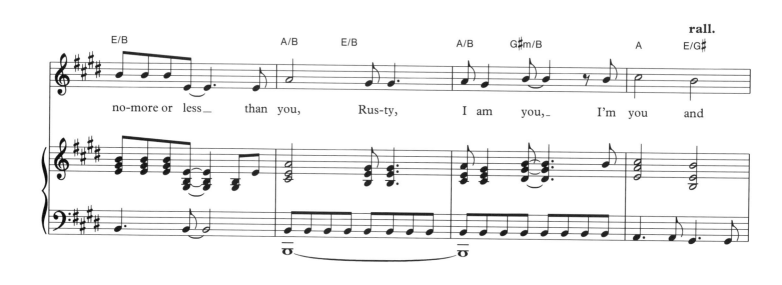

no-more or less ____ than you, Rus-ty, I am you, _ I'm you and

on - ly you, ____ have the po-wer with - in you, ____

I am the star - light, ____ I can a -

turn a-round and help you,_ if you draw on what is deep

turn a-round and help you,_ if you draw on what is deep

in - side.

in - side.

NEXT TIME YOU FALL IN LOVE

MUSIC BY ANDREW LLOYD WEBBER
LYRICS BY DON BLACK

guess I'm not too good at keep-ing love a-live for long,   I   think I've found the ans-wers but the
- times you turn a-way from what your heart tells you is right,   and   so you set-tle for what-ev-er

I've re-lived ev-ery mo-ment that I ev - er shared with you, what fools we were to end a dream that looked like com-ing true. Next time you fall in love_____ it bet - ter

ONE ROCK 'N' ROLL TOO MANY

MUSIC BY ANDREW LLOYD WEBBER
LYRICS BY RICHARD STILGOE

Easy rock tempo

One Rock 'n' Roll__ too ma - ny,__ one night's sleep too few.

Too much ring - ing that bell__ takes its toll out__ of you. The

sound's too loud, the light's too bright, my chains are too hea-vy and my pants are too tight.

One Rock 'n' Roll _ too ma - ny _ takes its toll _____ out of you.

One Rock 'n' Roll _ too ma - ny, one more fare - well show.

C'm-on. clap your hands, are you hav-ing a good _ time? _ (No!) Well my rave's

been raid-ed and my hip just hopped, my Mo-jo ain't work-ing and my

pill has just popped. One Rock 'n' Roll too ma-ny takes its toll

out of you.

poco accel.

One Rock 'n' Roll too ma-ny, I can't take no more.

LIGHT AT THE END OF THE TUNNEL

MUSIC BY ANDREW LLOYD WEBBER
LYRICS BY RICHARD STILGOE

Die-sel is for un-be-lie-vers, e-lec-tri-ci-ty is wrong,___ steam has got the po-wer that will

pull us a-long.___ There's a light at the end of the tun-nel, there's a

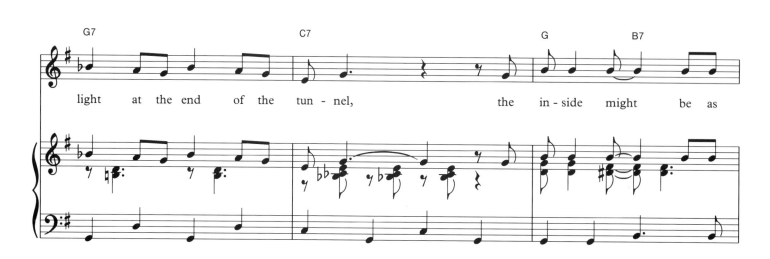

light at the end of the tun-nel, the in-side might be as

light at the end of the tun - nel, he saw the

light at the end of the tun - nel. Well thanks James Watt for

watch-ing that pot, __ he saw the light at the end of the tun - nel, he saw the

light at the end of the tun - nel, the in - side might be as

black as the night, but at the end of the tun-nel there's a light. There are

dark days__ a-head when the po-wer goes dead,__ when the oil runs dry,_____

what can we try? We could use the sun-light, but it don't shine at night,

nu-cle-ar fis - sion leaves a nas - ty e-mis-sion. Soon the pis-tons will be hum-ming,

steam will have a se-cond com-ing. We see the light at the

end of the tun-nel, we see the

light at the end of the tun-nel.

Just dig a hole___ and haul out the coal,___ we see the

Printed in Great Britain by Halstan & Co. Ltd., Amersham, Bucks.

5/97 (27670)